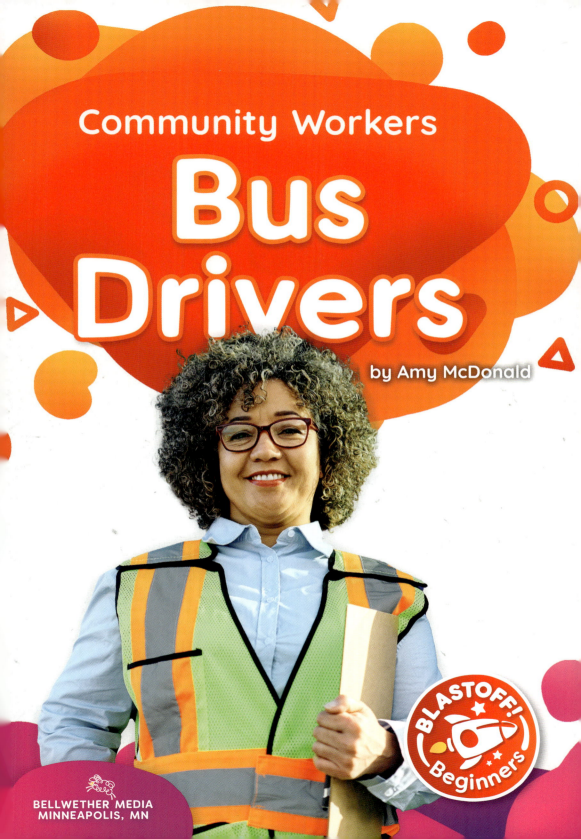

Blastoff! Beginners are developed by literacy experts and educators to meet the needs of early readers. These engaging informational texts support young children as they begin reading about their world. Through simple language and high frequency words paired with crisp, colorful photos, Blastoff! Beginners launch young readers into the universe of independent reading.

Sight Words in This Book

a	help	say	to
can	here	some	up
for	in	the	use
from	is	there	where
go	people	they	you

This edition first published in 2025 by Bellwether Media, Inc.

No part of this publication may be reproduced in whole or in part without written permission of the publisher. For information regarding permission, write to Bellwether Media, Inc., Attention: Permissions Department, 6012 Blue Circle Drive, Minnetonka, MN 55343.

Library of Congress Cataloging-in-Publication Data

LC record for Bus Drivers available at: https://lccn.loc.gov/2024004943

Text copyright © 2025 by Bellwether Media, Inc. BLASTOFF! BEGINNERS and associated logos are trademarks and/or registered trademarks of Bellwether Media, Inc. Bellwether Media is a division of Chrysalis Education Group.

Editor: Betsy Rathburn   Designer: Laura Sowers

Printed in the United States of America, North Mankato, MN.

Table of Contents

On the Job	4
What Are They?	6
What Do They Do?	12
Why Do We Need Them?	20
Bus Driver Facts	22
Glossary	23
To Learn More	24
Index	24

On the Job

The bus is here.
Hello, bus driver!

What Are They?

Bus drivers work in cities. Some work for schools.

They drive a **route**. They go from stop to stop.

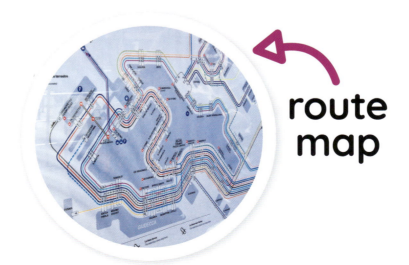

route map

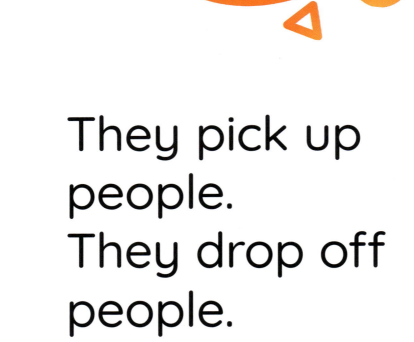

They pick up people.
They drop off people.

What Do They Do?

Bus drivers open doors. They say hello. Some take **fares**.

fare

They help people **board** the bus. Some use **lifts**.

They bring people places. Some drive to schools.

They follow driving rules. They keep riders safe!

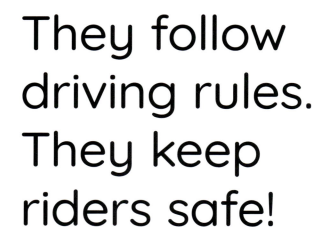

Why Do We Need Them?

Where to next? A bus driver can take you there!

Bus Driver Facts

Tools

route map

bus

lift

A Day in the Life

say hello

take fares

help people board

Glossary

board

to get on

fares

money given for rides

lifts

tools that carry people up and down

route

a path from one place to another

To Learn More

ON THE WEB

FACTSURFER

Factsurfer.com gives you a safe, fun way to find more information.

1. Go to www.factsurfer.com.

2. Enter "bus drivers" into the search box and click .

3. Select your book cover to see a list of related content.

Index

board, 14
bus, 4, 14
cities, 6
doors, 12
drive, 8, 16, 18
fares, 12
hello, 12
lifts, 14, 15

people, 10, 14, 16
riders, 18
route, 8
rules, 18
safe, 18
schools, 6, 16
stop, 8, 9

The images in this book are reproduced through the courtesy of: Drazen Zigic, front cover; Kadak, p. 3; Prostock-studio, pp. 4-5; Fly View Productions, pp. 6, 16-17; Richard Bradford, pp. 6-7; Alphotographic, p. 8 (route map); Wirestock Creators, pp. 8-9; Olesia Bilkei, pp. 10-11; xpixel, p. 12 (fare); AleksandarGeorgiev, pp. 12-13; Belish, pp. 14-15; SolStock, pp. 18-19; Vladimir Vladimirov, pp. 20-21; Regien Paassen, p. 22 (bus); vm, p. 22 (route map); Luckydoor, p. 22 (lift); SDI Productions, p. 22 (say hello); lena Chevalier, p. 22 (take fares); Peter Titmuss/ Alamy, p. 22 (help people board); Stuart Monk, p. 23 (board); cesarvr, p. 23 (fares); Jaren Jai Wicklund, p. 23 (lifts); Norman Pogson/ Alamy, p. 23 (route).